In Search of
Zulfiqar Ali Bhutto

Also, by the Author, on Amazon:

* In Search of Peace
* The Prisoner of Manora
  & Time to Die
* In Search of Truth (2nd Ed.)
* Learning How to Die
* In Search of Palestine

Scourge yourself if you don't know or ignore the tragedy of Palestine since the Balfour Declaration of November 1917: a tale of sorrow, oppression, humiliation, abuse, occupation, deprivation of basic needs, medicine, milk for infants, and unceasing killings.

I must keep fighting, until I am dying… Paul Robeson's Old Man River.

** Bacchus & Ishtar … stories*

In Search of
Zulfiqar Ali Bhutto

Baqi Muhammed-Ally

* Four-year old Mithi to Nana: *My Mommy knows everything,
I know everything, you know nothing.*

* Looking up from her drawing, *Nanee, do you understand Nana?
I can't understand him!*

Stage left: Nana doubling over in laughter (:-)

Table of Contents

* Preface ix

* ZAB Happenings 1
* The Star that Shines 5
* The Fall of Dacca 6
* The Finest Hour 7
* The Simla Acord 8
* The Nuclear Bomb 9
* ZAB and China 10
* Operation Fair Play 12
* Lights Out 14
* Do no Mischief 15
* The Sins of the Fathers 16

* Epitaph 18

Preface

For ever so long, ZAB has intrigued me. Who was this man? What did he achieve? What caused his downfall?

In some respects, this is an endeavour into uncharted territory because, as far as I can tell, there is no unbiased assessment of ZAB on record.

Please tell me what you think. Your views, if constructive, shall be defended as my own.

ZAB Happenings

<u>Summer of 1957</u>: I first met ZAB while visiting my father in Larkana where he was posted as the Additional District & Sessions Judge. After tennis at the local Gymkhana one hot afternoon, I tried to play billiards. To my horror, the cue slipped and tore a hole in the muddy pink felt top of the billiard table. After viewing the damage, the Club Secretary hoped that repair was possible instead of replacing the felt top. In either case, the cost would be added to my father's bill. *(And that was meant to comfort me?)*

Worry walked with me back to my father's house where house staff told me that I was wanted in the Autak (formal drawing room). Clad in soaking perspiration, t-shirt and shorts, I was introduced, *This is Mr Zulfiqar Ali Bhutto, he is a barrister from England.* (I didn't understand what a *barrister* was, didn't care, just wanted to get under a shower). Muttering something unintelligible, I fled.

<u>Intercontinental Hotel June/July 1966</u>: I was with a beautiful sari-clad woman at the Nasreen Room in my beloved city of Karachi. We were drinking Stingers when along came ZAB and asked my companion to dance. She signaled toward me, I nodded assent. After dancing to two numbers, they returned and I asked ZAB to join us for a drink. He sat, looked at me searchingly, then said, *I don't remember your name but you are from such and such family of Sindh and I met you at your father's house in Larkana in 1957.*

I was floored! In the dimly lit Nasreen Room, I was dressed to the nines in a dark suit, shell-pink shirt, and a Foulard tie, and to connect me to the callow stripling of 1957 in shorts and t-shirt was an amazing recall. I ordered him another Chivas Regal and said to myself, *Wow. What a guy!*

It was soon obvious that ZAB was smitten with the dark-eyed beauty and thus rose the green-eyed monster within. When the band took a break and the Akai reel came on, with an *excuse us* to ZAB, I swept the dark-eyed beauty to the dance floor.

<u>December 1957</u>: Taj Muhammad Khan Odho's father was the Sardar of the fierce Odho tribe in Jacobabad in Upper Sindh who had supported the Brits in their fight against the Hurs led by the Pagaro tribe. After the Sardar passed away, and for services he had rendered, young TMKO was made a Ward of the United Kingdom as he had no older living male member of the family. After schooling, he trained as a fighter pilot at Loughborough outside London during WWII. When it ended, we find TMKO (now known as Prince Odho or Bob), in a 17-foot yellow Lincoln Continental leading a giddy club-life while, back at Jacobabad, his mother, Ayee Sahiba, oversaw the running of the paddy fields to send him the wherewithal for his lifestyle. Finally, he returned to Karachi in 1957 and rented an apartment in Hussain D'Silva Park.

<u>Night & Day in 1958</u>: At an American School sock-hop, Bob's son, Pir Muhammad Khan Odho, aka Paul, said, *Dad's having a party. Let's go there.* We were blasted with Frances Faye belting out her classic Night & Day: loved that song ever since. Bob gave me a taped copy at our farewell-to-D-133 Clifton house in July 1988.

<u>The Hand-Curse in 1964</u>: I had graduated to being invited by Bob to his parties and one evening, Illahi Bux Soomro, on entering Bob's flat was greeted by ZAB with Lakh-La-Laanat (a shaming Hand-Curse in Sindh). Now, IBS, being a scion of an old Sindh dynasty, which had

governed Sindh for over two centuries, was not going to take the insult unchallenged and promptly returned the compliment. It was clear from his darkening visage that ZAB was not pleased. Not long after he took over as President in December 1971, IBS was imprisoned. (I met him in chains and shackles at the High Court of Sindh in 1972). ZAB did not forget slights by whomsoever: a clear and fearful message to his detractors. In 1973, however, a rapprochement took place and ZAB sent IBS as Minister to the Pakistan High Commission in Britain. (Guess the latter had apologized).

<u>June/July 1968</u>: At Ahmed Pirbhai's invitation to his new home on Tipu Sultan Road, my wife and I arrived late and were shown into a long rectangular room where an expensive radiogram played Urdu ghazals. In the far corner sat ZAB, his wife Nusrat, and Rafi and Jackie Muneer. ZAB was holding forth except that some choice epithets against the-then President Ayub Khan crept into his grammar. (Was it because he had been replaced as Minister for Foreign Affairs after disagreeing with the President over the Tashkent Accord of 1966?) Anyhow, I called out, *Piroo, please tell Saeen that there are ladies present.* ZAB walked over, looked me long in the face then walked back. But the language quality improved.

<u>December 1970</u>: Zain and Marzieh Hidayetullah's invitation for dinner at the Sindh Club, found us having drinks in the Ladies Bar when in walked ZAB flush with his Pakistan People's Party winning 81 of the 132 seats in the former West Pakistan (WP) in the December 1970 election held under the aegis of the Martial Law Administrator and President General Yahya Khan. Mujeeb-ur-Rahman's Awami League, however, swept the polls in the former East Pakistan (EP) winning 167 of the 169 seats and was thus entitled to nominate the Prime Minister of undivided Pakistan. (More on this later).

On entering the Ladies Bar, ZAB saw a mid-level bureaucrat and called out, *Qamruzzaman Shah, I told you I would win.* Then he joined Nusrat,

Rafi and Jackie Muneer, Ghulam Mustafa Jatoi (a stalwart of the PPP) and Mr Dingomal Ramchandani, a respected senior lawyer of Karachi. On ZAB's approach, Mr R stood up and offered ZAB his seat and … ZAB took it! Somewhat taken aback, I wondered: ZAB had done his pupillage in Mr R's chambers, so …

<u>Early 1971</u>: Abdullah Haroon (later knighted by the British), was a senior member of the Muslim League from Sindh which had fought for the independence of Pakistan from undivided India under the leadership of Muhammad Ali Jinnah. One of his three sons, Mahmood Haroon, was nominated by President Yahya Khan as High Commissioner to the United Kingdom. Ahmed Pirbhai hosted a gala dinner at his residence and a ton of people were invited as well as several leading lights of the PPP resplendent in their custom-tailored black suits with the sherwani collar embroidered in gold thread.

Looking for a washroom, I was walking up a grand staircase when I met Mir Rasool Bux Talpur whose ancestors had ruled Sindh from 1783 to 1843 until Rear Admiral Sir Frederick Maitland blew up their out-moded batteries on the peninsula of Manora outside Karachi. Four years later, Sindh became the last province in undivided India to fall.

I said, *Mir Saheb, what are you doing in the Piyo Pillao Party* (Drink and Give me Drink Party). Mir Saheb just smiled.

The Star that Shines

Later that evening, an old friend, Gul Lakhwani, and I were having a drink at a bamboo bar on the lawns of Piroo's house. A few feet away, were ZAB, Nusrat, Ghulam Mustafa Jatoi, Keeks, and Rafi and Jackie Muneer. Spotting Gul, ZAB called out to him. In sotto voce, I urged Gul not to go but he did and ZAB asked him to read his palm. Gul had more than a smattering knowledge of palmistry and after a few minutes of examining our hero's palm said, *your star shines brilliantly but I don't see it after 1981.*

In an enraged voice, ZAB called out, *Piroo, lock up this Banya in the bathroom.* Poor Gul walked back, shoulders sagging. I hugged him. But as events proved, Gul was only two years off as ZAB's star vanished in April 1979.

Idhar Hum Udhar Tum (*me here, you there*): Did this ZAB mantra inspire Yahya Khan's ambition to continue as President over the quarreling Mujeeb and ZAB? Perhaps, but East Pakistanis were not having it as Mujeeb was entitled to become the Prime Minister. Trouble erupted, army action ensued, killings happened. The Governor of EP, Admiral Ahsan resigned and so did the GOC, Sahibzada Yakub Khan, because they did not agree to the army action. Thus, General Tikka Khan was dispatched and he used even more bullets resulting in a lot of East Pakistanis fleeing into India.

The Fall of Dacca

Indira Gandhi, the Prime Minister of India, was aghast. She ordered the Indian Army C-in-C, Field Martial Sam Hormusji Manekshaw, to take action. He sent his troops into EP and on December 16 1971, General 'Tiger' Niazi of the Pakistan Army surrendered his sword to General J S Aurora of India and 93,000 Pakistani soldiers were taken prisoner. (Tiger?)

Dacca's Fall can never be forgotten. It seared the heart. Gloom found a mirror on every face, people sobbed on the streets. Then, I recalled an evening in 1967-68 at the Sindh Club Bridge Room when a retired Captain burst out with *Pakistan has four colonies, Bradford, Birmingham, Manchester and East Pakistan.* Startled, I said, *Captain, what are you saying? That's not right.* He ignored me.

But such an attitude was unfortunately prevalent in some quarters and it was, therefore, not surprising that during the run-up to the December 1970 election Mujeeb decried the fact that EP did not derive any benefit from jute exports though it was mostly grown in and exported from EP.

Harking back to the 1948 election held after Partition and we find that **all of the winners from East Pakistan were West Pakistanis!** So, there you have it. We wronged East Pakistan!

Bangladesh came into being. We were left to lick our wounds.

The Finest Hour

Yahya Khan had had enough. He handed over the Presidency to ZAB on December 20, 1971. Soon thereafter, one evening, a dazed and subdued people saw ZAB on Pakistan TV. He lifted us with soothing words, morale boosting words, applied salve to our wounds, and gave us hope ... I saw people begin to crack a smile at his tuneless screech of Sohni Dharti (beautiful land), women wiped their tears surreptitiously. It was his finest hour. And while I was never a ZAB-follower, I admired him that evening. *What a guy!*

The Simla Accord

ZAB went to India and did a Veni, Vidi, Vici. He charmed Indian Prime Minister, Indira Gandhi, into releasing the 93,000 soldiers taken prisoner at the Fall of Dacca. (She was probably happy to be rid of them as their maintenance cost must have been huge). A Peace Treaty was executed on July 02, 1972 to the effect that all differences between the two countries would be settled through bilateral negotiations. And this obviously included Kashmir, the biggest and thorniest bone of contention between India and Pakistan. (Did I say bone? Gosh darn it, I meant the whole cow!) If only that Treaty were subsisting …

This was a fitting encore to ZAB's Finest Hour and had he been a Roman Emperor, he would have been driven back home in a golden chariot to an exultant fanfare of trumpets. *What a guy*!

Tribute must also be paid to the vision and sagacity of Indira Gandhi who clearly wanted India and Pakistan to settle their differences peacefully. Alas!

The Nuclear Bomb

On July 24, 1972, ZAB committed Pakistan to go nuclear. That he was far sighted in this regard, is evident from what he had said earlier in 1965 when he was the Foreign Minister: *If India builds the bomb, we will eat grass or leaves, even go hungry, but we will get our own.*

India's tested nuclear in 1974 but it was not until May 1998 that Pakistan exploded its first nuclear devices. Even though ZAB had been *swung* off the earth courtesy General Zia-ul-Haq, it was ZAB who inspired the nuclear journey. *What a guy!*

ZAB and China

That he re-structured Pakistan's foreign affiliations and put China at the head was also one of ZAB's signal achievements. Together with China's Foreign Minister, Chou En Lai, the Pakistan-China relationship was formed on a much-favoured basis which has endured ever since.

What a guy!

Before ZAB became President, Richard Nixon's National Security Advisor, Henry Kissinger, visited Pakistan on July 09, 1971. That the latter came down with a cold was a ruse as he actually went to China to meet its leaders. This was the precursor to Nixon's much-heralded visit to China on February 21, 1972. And so, the bamboo curtain began to rise. (Lest we forget Pakistan and Romania each played a part in such achievement).

A reference to Ronald Reagan in regard to China is necessary here though it may strike some as a *non-sequitur*. On October 25, 1971 the UN General Assembly voted to admit the People's Republic of China and expel Taiwan. The recently released Nixon tapes revealed Reagan, a Taiwan supporter, saying in a telephone call the next day to Richard Nixon: *Look at the monkeys from Africa* (delegation from Tanzania) *jumping up and down at China's entry into the UN … damn them, they are not even comfortable wearing shoes.* (Reagan was then the Governor of California).

Noam Chomsky called the United States a *very racist society* and Ronald Reagan as a prime example of a *very racist man* during an interview with GRITtv about Ferguson-related issues and race relations. (Cheryl K Chumley – The Washington Times – Thursday, December 11, 2014).

Part 2 of Reagan's Showtime Review reveals that he supported the apartheid regimes of South Africa and Rhodesia and employed racist code words, such as *jungle roads, welfare queens, States Rights.*

Ignoble words, discreditable attitude and conduct, you might say. But which still find favour half a century later with Donald Trump and his votaries and towel bearers in the Republican party who do not live up to the party's strong and dignified elephant symbol, who propagate Trump's lies about the 2020 election, and who contort, concoct, and suppress the truth. With the exception of a few, such is now the measure of the Grand Old Party.

Operation Fair Play

ZAB hand-picked General Zia-ul-Haq as COAS of the Pakistan Army by having him supersede several senior Generals. He obviously thought it would beget him life-long loyalty. Guess it was the worst mistake he ever made!

The 1977 election resulted in a landslide victory for ZAB but the opposition cried foul. Rigging was alleged and the Pakistan National Alliance came into being and comprised a hoi-polloi of people and parties. Strikes immobilized the country. Talks failed. Eventually, General Zia led a bloodless coup and ZAB was ousted from his Prime Ministerial bed around midnight on July 05, 1977. Not long after, he was charged with having caused the killing of Ahmed Raza Kasuri's father in a car ambush though the son Raza was, allegedly, the target. A Kafkaesque trial ensued in the Lahore High Court, ZAB was found guilty and sentenced to death. On Appeal to the Supreme Court of Pakistan, four of the seven judges aligned against him. To no one's surprise the appeal was dismissed and the sentence confirmed. This caused the resignation of three judges, Dorab Patel, Fakhruddin Ebrahim and A B Haleem, who were from Sindh, and who declared that in a 4-3 verdict, the death sentence was customarily commuted to life imprisonment.

World leaders from all over urged Zia to exercise clemency and commute the death sentence but he would not have it because to quell military adventurers, the 1973 Constitution had made its abrogation treasonous.

And Zia knew that even from a prison cell ZAB could have inspired a great deal of unbearable agitation against him. Thus, he could not let ZAB live.

The Dawn newspaper of April 04, 1979 showed some white-out pages with a black-bordered snippet that ZAB had been hanged at Kot Lakhpat Jail in Rawalpindi. Gloom descended upon Pakistan, much like that upon the sailors after the killing of the albatross*. People were stunned, frozen by so gross and callous an act. Several senior PPP members/officials were also arrested.

---

* The Rime of the Ancient Mariner by S T Coleridge

Lights Out

The man awoke in the dark. What was this heavy weight? Was he having a heart attack? He couldn't move. *Someone was sitting on his chest* ... his mind cried out. Someone was holding down his legs. He screamed, *Choro*. Instead, hands clasped his throat, he struggled, choked, it became darker ...

Through the mist of his near-closed eyelids, he saw and felt his unshod feet raking the stony ground, then he was lifted up some stairs and a dark bag enveloped his world. Something round and cable-like, was fitted round his neck and then it dawned ... *what, no, you can't ... I did not kill Kasuri's father ...*

A sudden yank, a fall, and the life of a brilliant man of Pakistan was brutally and unmercifully taken with a shuddering of his feet.**

____

** How exactly ZAB met his end is shrouded in some mystery. One story has it that he was carried to the gallows on a stretcher which supports the view that he was first strangled. The above is the author's dramatization.

Do no Mischief

On the earth after *it has been set in* order: Ch. 7:56, The Holy Qur'an. Chapters 2:11 and 2:60 are to similar effect.

All of the principal characters in this story ZAB, Zia-ul-Haq, Mujeeb-ur-Rahman and Indira Gandhi met with violent deaths.

Mujeeb was assassinated on July 15, 1975 by young Bangladesh Army officers. ZAB was hanged on April 04, 1979, Indira Gandhi was assassinated by two of her Sikh bodyguards on October 31, 1984 at her residence in New Delhi and Zia-ul-Haq's C-130 Hercules aircraft crashed 2/3 minutes after takeoff from Bahawalpur on August 17, 1988. Did they do *mischief?*

The Sins of the Fathers

Are visited upon the children? Exodus 34:7, Numbers 14:18, Deuteronomy 5:9, etc., say so and so far as ZAB, Mujeeb and Indira are concerned, their children also met with violent deaths.

Factually, all three of Mujeeb's sons, Kamal, Jamal and Russel, and other members of his family were killed during the coup of July 15, 1975 except for his two daughters, Hasina and Rehana who were then in Germany.

ZAB's younger son Shahnawaz died mysteriously in Nice, France, on July 08, 1985, believed to be poisoned though Zia's government claimed it was a drug overdose. Mir Murtaza, ZAB's older son, was cut down by a hail of bullets about 100 meters from the Bhutto residence at 70 Clifton in Karachi on September 20, 1996. Taken to the Mideast Hospital, he lay on a gurney unattended despite bleeding, then he died. And Benazir was assassinated on December 27, 2007 after a political rally at Liaqat National Bagh in Rawalpindi when she stood through the sunroof of her Toyota Land Cruiser. The only survivor of ZAB's family is his younger daughter, Sanam, who escaped to Britain.

Indira Gandhi's younger son and heir, Sanjay, died on June 23, 1980 when the light plane he was piloting crashed soon after takeoff. On May 21 1991, her older son, Rajiv, while campaigning for a second term as Prime Minister, was approached by a woman, Dhanu, who touched his feet then detonated an explosive belt below her dress. It was later learnt that she was a member of the Tamil Tigers.

Zia-ul-Haq: As the story goes, the only piece of his identifiable body was his jaw-bone which was buried in Islamabad in a square since referred to as Jhabra Chowk (Jaw-bone square). Pakistan is still suffering from his wrong-doings but that story is for another day.

Epitaph

Like a meteor ZAB blazed across the Pakistan sky and like a meteor he tailed off. What was his North Star? What was his measure?

* A highly accomplished visionary, ZAB started Pakistan's nuclear journey. Had he not done so, Pakistan would have been hogtied by India in multiple ways. The United States still holds the start-up of Pakistan's nuclear venture against ZAB.

* Trail-blazed Pakistan's relationship with China; applied balm to Pakistan's soul when Dacca fell; extricated 93,000 soldiers from India and achieved the brilliant Simla Accord together with Indira Gandhi.

* Disagreed strongly with views not his own. Exacted vengeance upon his detractors or those who supposedly slighted him.

* Worst legacies: the nationalization of education and financial institutions.

* A contradiction in many respects: he was caring but arrogant, intelligent but emotional, verbose but charming, freed the labour class dressed in Saville Row suits with a Mao cap on his head. In other words, he was human. Who amongst us has not experienced some of these attributes? Those who deny are either faking or seek sainthood.

I was never a ZAB follower but today I weep for him. If only …

Lord, you gave me a mountain, A mountain that I can never climb

… Elvis Presley